STEPHEN COX

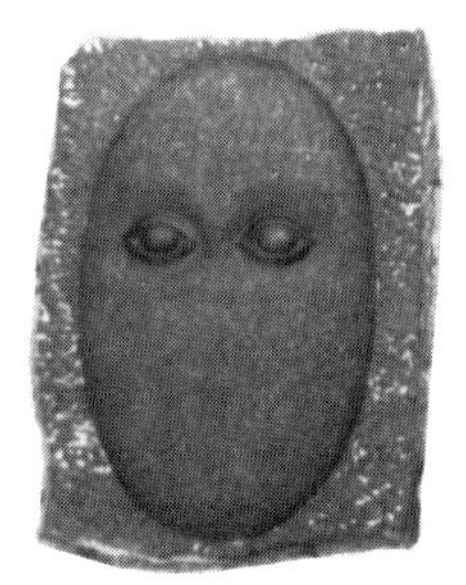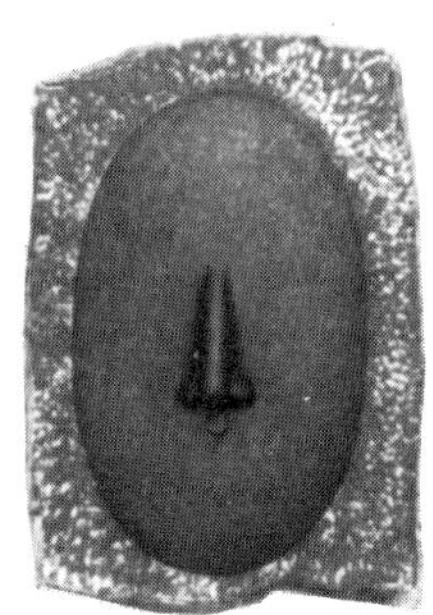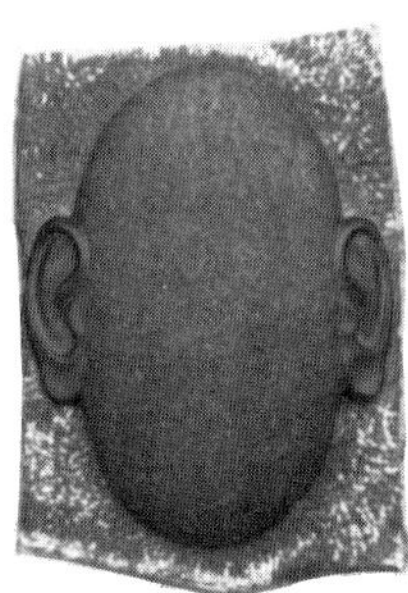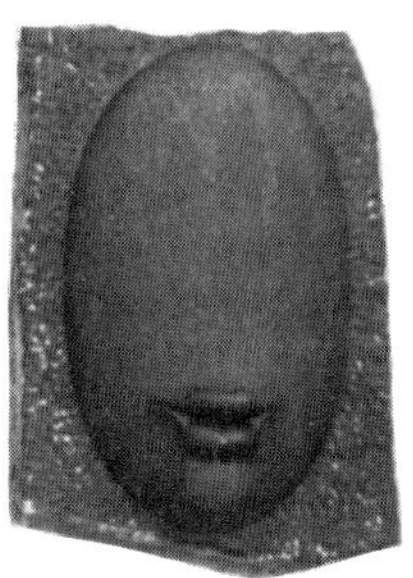

THE TATE GALLERY

Front cover: **Tanmatras** 1985 (detail)

Photographs: Eileen Tweedy; Cherian Bros, Madras; Prabjit Singh; the artist.
Photograph on page 11 courtesy Queensland Art Gallery, Australia.

This exhibition is sponsored by Gerald Metals Limited

ISBN 0 946590 47 8
Published by order of the Trustees 1986
for the exhibition of 30 July–19 October 1986
Copyright © 1986 The Tate Gallery All rights reserved
Published by Tate Gallery Publications, Millbank, London SW1P 4RG
Printed by Jolly & Barber Ltd, Rugby, Warwickshire

FOREWORD

This catalogue was first published by the British Council to accompany the exhibition by Stephen Cox that comprised the British section of the Sixth Indian Triennale in Delhi, February–March 1986. Cox was awarded a major prize for this work. We are republishing the catalogue by kind permission of the British Council, with some additional material discussing the most recent pieces.

Cox's sculptures attracted a great deal of attention in India, not only because of their intrinsic qualities, but because they were made in the sub-continent, and reflect the artist's reaction to a powerful sculptural tradition. Most of the pieces that were shown in Delhi are in the exhibition at the Tate Gallery, together with newer sculptures, some begun in India and completed here.

Our thanks are due first of all to the artist without whom there would be no exhibition. We are also grateful to the British Council who arranged and funded Cox's period of work in India while he was making the pieces shown in Delhi. The exhibition was organised by the Fine Arts Department and by the Council's officers in Delhi and Madras all of whom have been equally helpful to the Tate Gallery. The Government College of Sculpture and Architecture, Mahabalipuram acted as host to Stephen Cox by arrangement with the Directorate of Technical Education of the Government of Tamil Nadu and the Tamil Nadu Tourism Department. Finally, we should like to thank Gerald Metals Limited for their support.

The catalogue was written by Michael Compton who acted as adviser to the British Council for the show.

Alan Bowness
Director

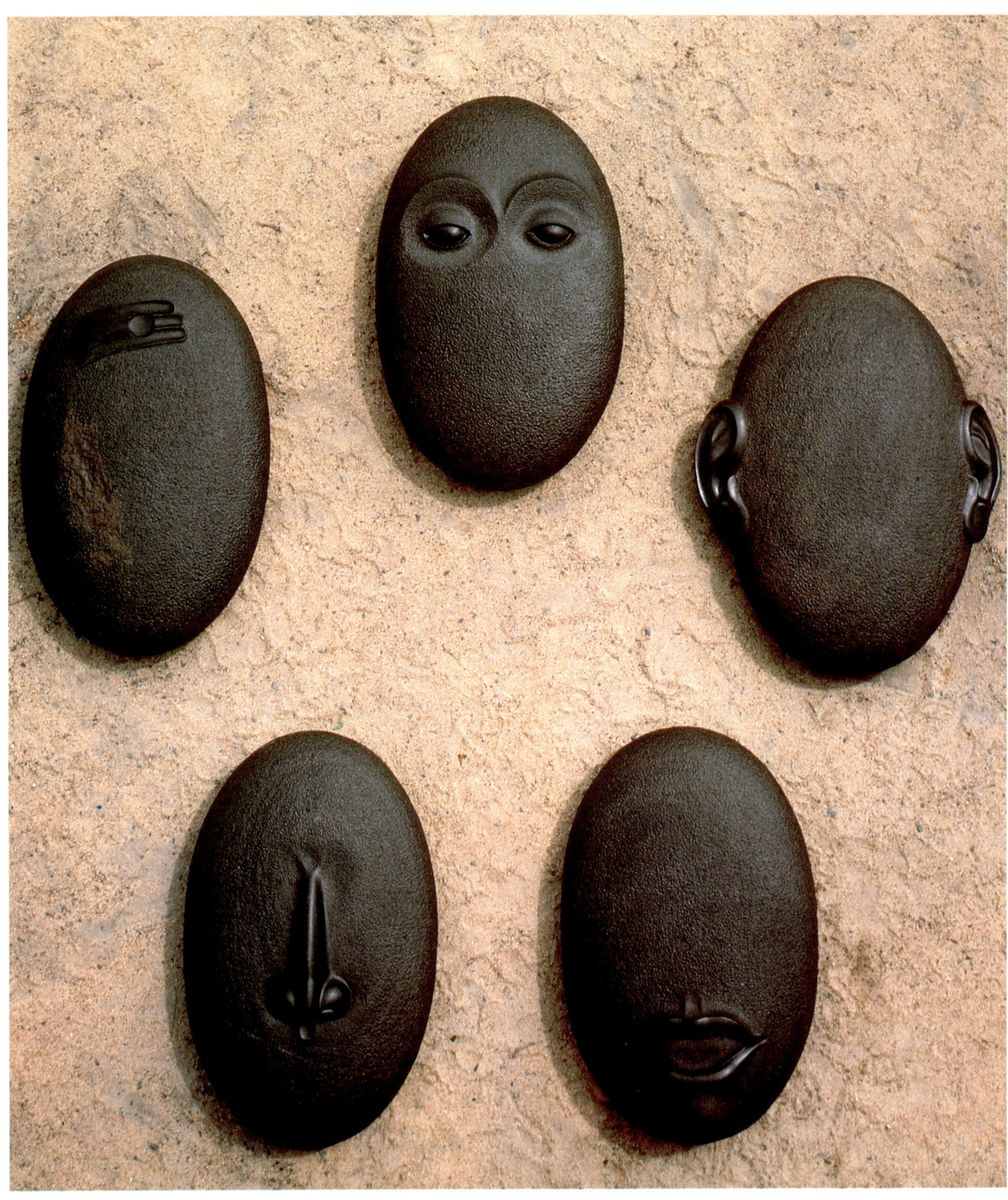

Tanmatras 1985
304.8 × 304.8 × 22.9 cm
Granite

THE ART OF STEPHEN COX

by Michael Compton

Art is unimaginable without a matrix of culture, even a parochial culture; it is inconceivable without a history; it cannot be separated from the properties of the materials of which it is made and these are themselves provided by that culture, history and by the physical world its peoples inhabit. All of these are elements of the web of language in which an art is expressed. At the same time, art is unimaginable without the artist and it is nothing without the instant comprehension that the work of art is a new thing, created, and inexpressible in words. I believe that Stephen Cox's work as a sculptor declares all this with as much strength as any contemporary art and it has come to represent the fullness of its mystery. For there is indeed a mystery. A work of art is a thing in itself having substance, power and presence; yet it is a sign or a symbol, a manifestation or a representation.

Western art of the last hundred years and more has often sought one simplification or another in order to lay open some element of the mystery and Cox himself has done this. But in the last eight years he has rebuilt his art out of old, new and purely personal elements in such a way that fissures and sutures in his structure are as potent as its perfections.

My own understanding of Cox's work has been built up, little by little, in the ordinary way, as I have seen pieces over the years, but its point of departure was one particular meeting. In 1976 I had seen some of his works in a show at the Lisson Gallery in London, and wanted to recommend him to the Biennale in Paris (a young artists exhibition). Cox's works comprised free standing plaster walls, placed in front of, and obscuring, the real walls of the galleries in which they stood. I saw them in relation

Relief: Mirror I 1979, Cement and plaster installation, Palazzo Reale, Milan

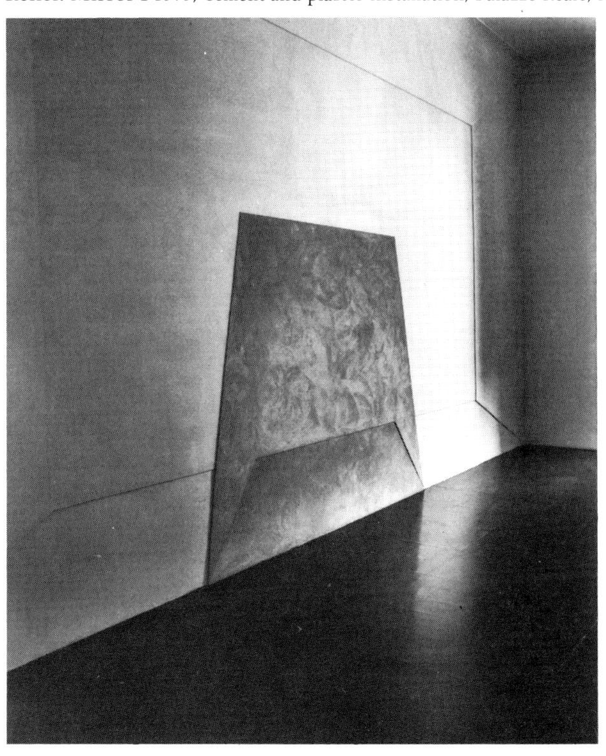

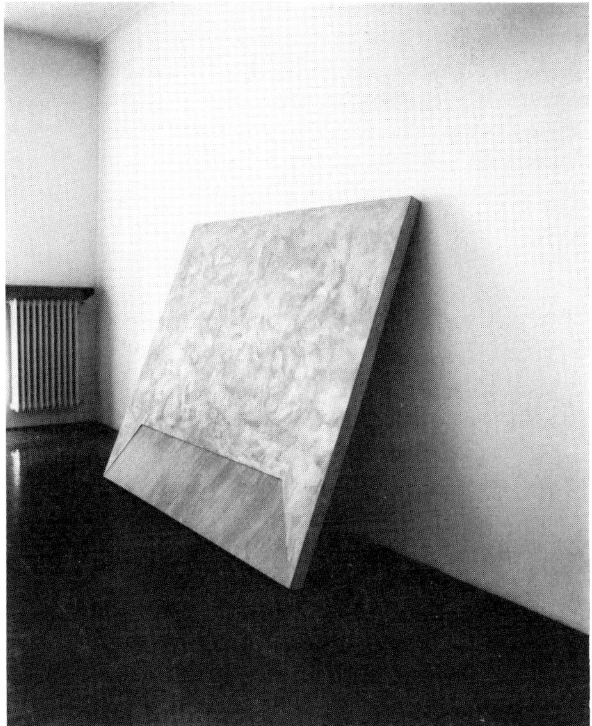

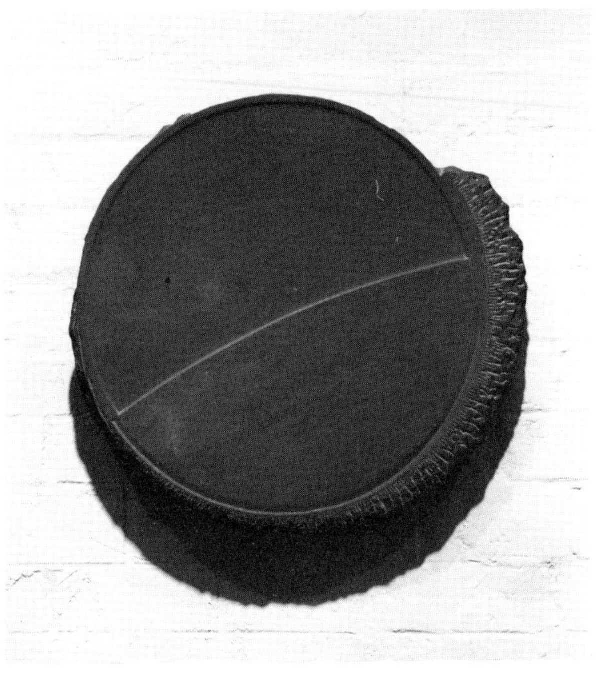

Tondo: Untitled 1980
39 × 48 cm
Forest of Dean stone
Contemporary Art Society, London

to 'Minimal' and 'Conceptual' art, and dealt with them according to my own habits – as quasi-linguistic devices. I certainly associated the pieces with a previous exhibition of wall-works by minimal and conceptual artists, also held at the Lisson Gallery. Several of these had seemed to turn on the idea that a drawing directly on the surface of a wall could not be removed and treated as a commodity; that by being integral it possessed and was possessed by the architecture which it marked out. On the other hand, in Cox's work a 'wall' was created and set apart from the real wall; it was no longer integral, certainly not permanent, and it was not marked. It was conceivably portable but still not negotiable as a commodity. It was however, like much Conceptual art, made in and for the space it occupied. I thought again of the white paintings of Robert Rauschenberg which had been drawn on only by the lights and the shadows of passers-by; also of the walls which I had seen built by Doug Wheeler, that had been dematerialised by a fringe of fluorescent light from hidden sources. Cox's plaster seemed on the contrary fully materialised by its fringes of corner-reinforcing strips and by the plaster which had been drawn over them forming an irregular return, however small, in relation to the dominant surface.

There wasn't much in the studio except bags of plaster, some other materials and a few earlier works. Cox talked at first diffidently. He had been concerned with proportion and scale as irreducible elements of sculpture. A very large piece, in several oblong panels, had been inscribed with a line representing the width of these panels within the height. But it seemed that measuring might become an obsessive device and should be eliminated as being too personal. Cox was emphatic that these works were sculpture, even though they did not enclose three-dimensional form. All that was enclosed was the void between the work and the wall behind. Cox had made a sculpture on the basis of what had become the specific field of painting: the two-dimensional, normally rectilinear, plane, so reclaiming it for his own medium. He had, moreover, created colour, without spreading any layer of paint. Cox spoke of the specific character, tint and density of local plasters. He explained how the timing and movement of the plasterer, with his tools in his hand, could create a subtle range of colours and textures which would only appear as the plaster dried hours later.

Here was a kind of art, apparently very restricted in form and technique, but, conversely, very rich in reference and evocative power. It remained, in spite of all considerations, very visual in mode and independent of attempts to rationalise it.

Cox was selected for the Biennale and showed a piece of the type I had seen at the Lisson Gallery. He chose to print in the catalogue a short text by John Hayes:

'The production of Stephen Cox's work is the appropriation and the objectification of the basic code of sculptural form.

The initial praxis is centred on the embodiment of surface as one element of the code and represents part of a more total and ongoing process both to individuate and also to interrelate other elements.'

From this point on Cox began to reconstruct an art of sculpture. At first the content and references were enriched more rapidly than the syntactic elements. Cox read the critical writings of Adrian Stokes which he seems to have valued in terms of the 'Art and Language' concern with the work of art as manifestation of culture, contingent on economic and social conditions. However, Stokes is rhapsodic, psychoanalytic, and full of the ro-

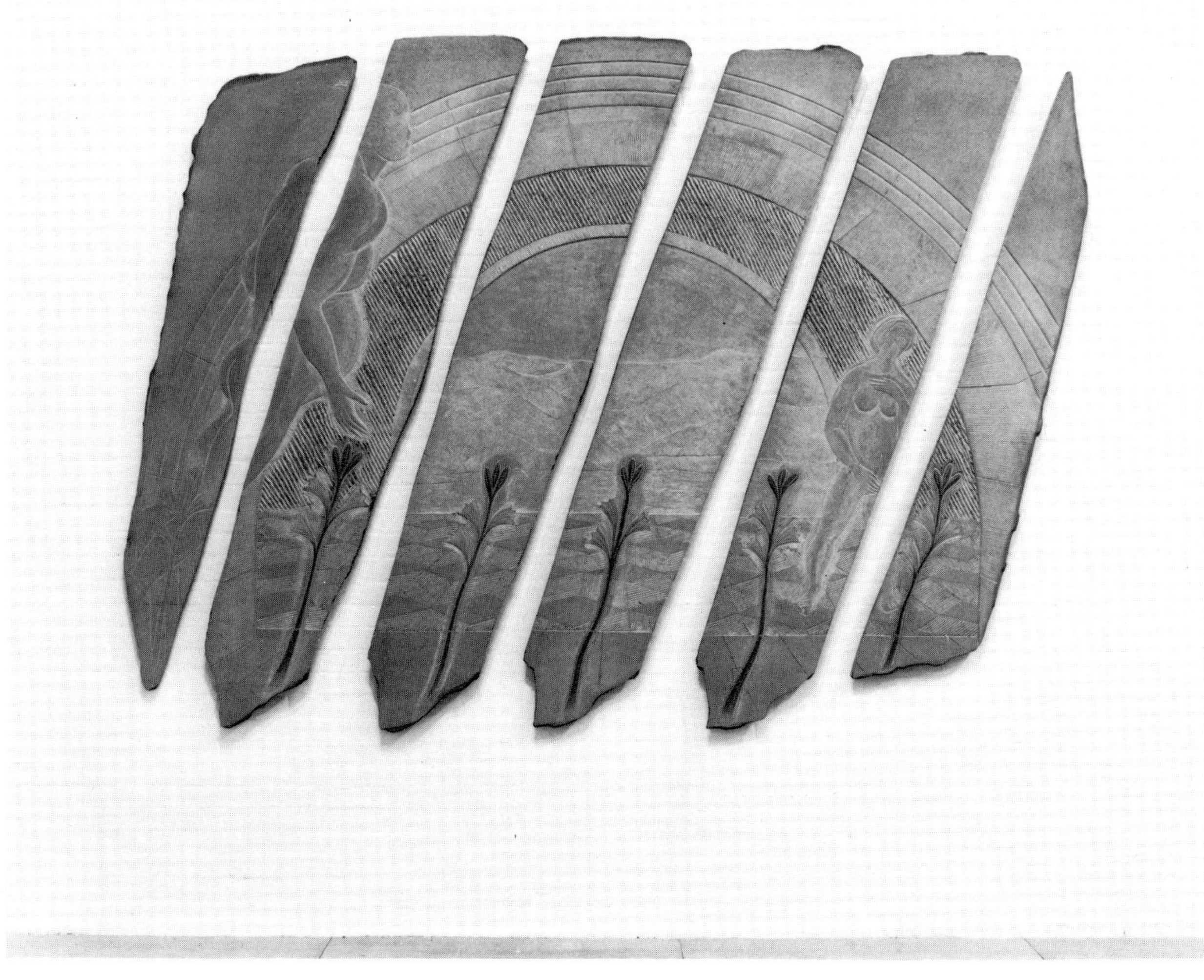

mance of place and history. The relation of art to its matrix is magical. Stokes writes of the Mediterranean region; on one page: 'the grape, the olive and the fig are yet the symbol of man's common need. Jehovah still walks his garden of myrtle, laurel, arbutus, cistus, juniper, evergreen-oak and wild olive, follows conduit paths in the cool of the evening,' but a few pages later: 'Jerusalem, with a mean annual rainfall of 26 inches, saw its precipi-tation fluctuate from 43 inches in 1877 to 12.5 inches in 1869'. His magic, like all good magic, is focused in things and in facts.

Cox found here a mirror of his own preoccupations. Stokes had written passionately of limestone, the deposit of billions of aquatic structures, subtly tinctured by minerals, by crystalline structure, by the water that had eroded it and was bonded within it. Cox had worked in

Tondo: **We Must Always Turn South** 1981
80 cm diameter
Verona of St. Ambrosia marble
Tate Gallery, London

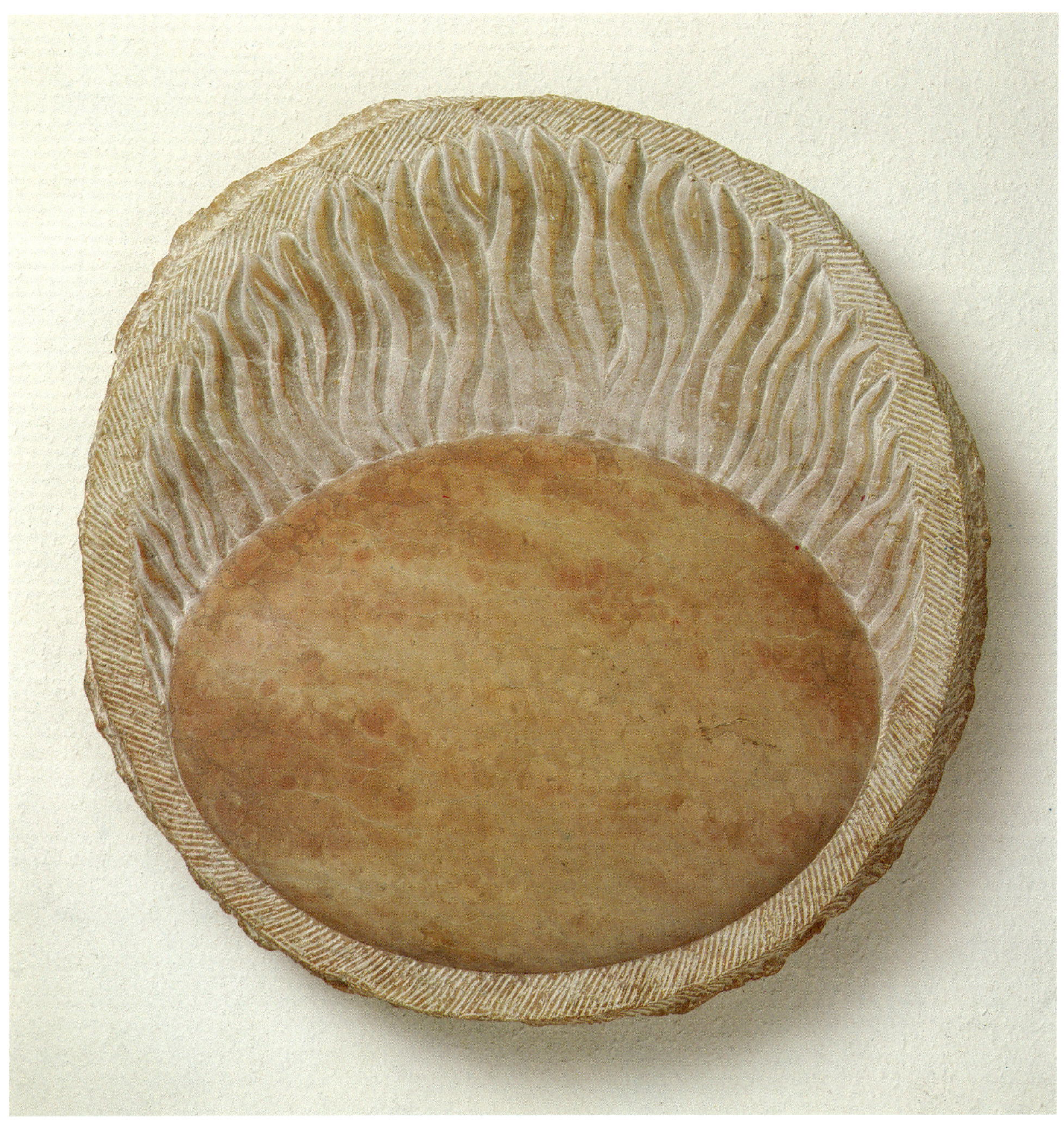

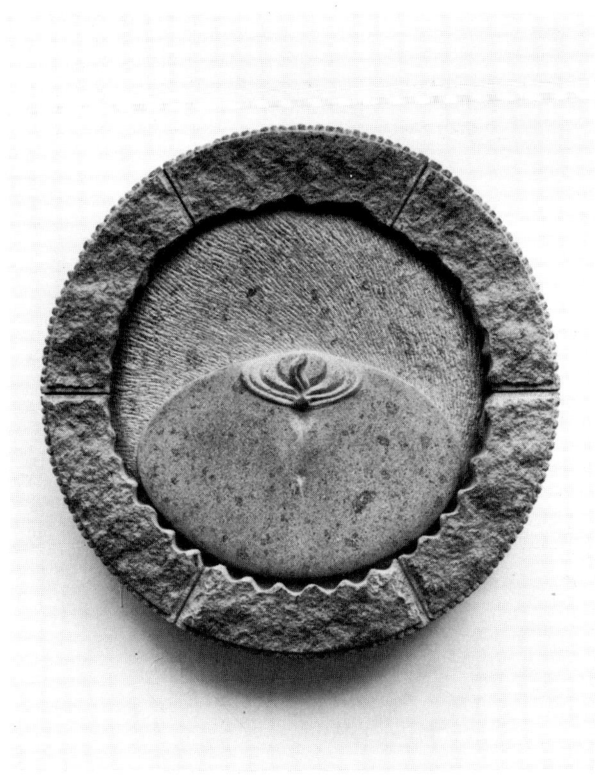

plaster, a burnt form of another geological deposit, re-formed by water and tinted in the same way by mineral impurities, by structure and bound water. Stokes had written especially of *schiacciato*, that is, a very low relief, the point at which the sculpture of the early Renaissance most closely approached painting, and, at the same time, adhered most closely to architecture. Cox had already reduced his relief to the pure surface.

He began again to make lines and very subtle tiltings of plane. They contained a very immediate reference to that science of perspective which had governed architecture, painting and sculpture in the early fifteenth century. He named his pieces after the heroes: 'Donato', 'Alberti'. He permitted and, indeed, emphasised illusion in his sculpture. He broke through the limits of the art of his period.

A series of slab-like works are engraved with a trapezium, rising from the lower edge in such a way that, as the slabs tilt between floor and wall, the trapezium appears as a shallow stage, filling the hidden ground between that edge and the line where the wall rises from the floor. We have a simple fusion of sculpture and architecture by means of a graphic device. The illusion is, of course, not permitted to be complete, but the work places the space of the viewer (his viewpoint) in relation to the basics of architectural structure. Cox did not seek the Renaissance ideal of the complete logical reconstruction of the world or the harmonious reordering of it. Although he had only a year earlier taken the classical position of the modernist, of narrowing the definition of his art, now, by the addition of a few lines, he pointed the way to an art, like that of the Renaissance and of many other rich cultures, transgressing the boundaries of media while comprehending them. Moreover he visited and then began to work continuously in Italy. He read the late Renaissance accounts by Giorgio Vasari of the marble and stone quarries and went to each. His materials became Mediterranean and he backed his work up with Mediterranean legends and history.

From this year, 1978, Cox's sculptural language grew rapidly. Rather than attempting to analyse this as if it were a spoken or written language, in terms of vocabulary, grammar, syntax, figures of speech and personal preferences I will try to hint at the richness of his art by picking out only a few of the themes and devices which he has developed.

First of all, Cox's art is an art of transformation. He has understood this essential fact which characterises sculpture more precisely than the other arts and brings it close to magic. He feels and respects the way that rocks embody the geological transformations of vastly distant pasts, whether volcanic, sedimentary or metamorphic. He leaves the clues to be read even in his finished pieces – the colours and crystalline or amorphous structure of the rock, the weathered edges, the planes of cleavage, the toolmarks of the quarry, and then his own toolmarks, polishings and chemical processes. All are signs of transformation which acknowledge a former state while creating the new.

He frequently employs ambiguity, a kind of reversible, because mental, transformation. For example, the perspectival lines on his leaning slabs of *c.*1978 may be considered as projections but they may also be considered as mirrors. The forms sketched in may seem to lie, that is, in front of rather than behind the relief. Another series took the ambiguity of perspective in a new direction. He produced a group of reliefs in the form of 'Tondos', that is, circular, dish-like forms, often made in the Italian early Renaissance. The medium of the relief is important to Cox because it expresses most clearly the unity of sculpture and architecture, even, potentially, the dominance of architecture by sculpture. But it also permits a pictorial use of space: such illusions as I have described above. Within the discs, Cox repeatedly described an oval rising from the bottom that could be seen as the perspectival projection of such a disc on the horizontal plane. The relief, hanging grittily and massively on the wall, could become a window or a mirror. The oval, seen on the surface, could be itself a pregnant form: an egg, a breast, a fruit, a mountain, a pool. Cox may allow it to be any or all of these or pin it down to one with a touch of detail.

Cox's sense of sculpture as a transformation of the stone has allowed him to decorate more freely than many other sculptors. He makes use of margins, of hatching, stippling, repeated rhythmic cuts. Here is another hint of his willingness to transgress the limits of current, pure sculpture – to bring into play the possibilities of other arts.

Colour has always been important to Cox; in this he is not exceptional as a sculptor but his progression has been unique. Even when he was working in plaster, as I have said, the intrinsic variety of colour was important to him, inseparable as it was from the medium and its mode of working. When he came to work in stone, the flatness of his surfaces drew attention to the watery, and perhaps water-created, tints in the dark grey of Forest of Dean stone. The spectacular colours of certain Italian marbles and limestones introduced a new wealth of colour. One device he has used creates colour by means of surface texture only. A polished stone (of a suitable kind) will be saturated in colour since the light penetrates the surface; but a surface that has been scratched or ground will become whiter with the scattering of light which cannot penetrate; chisel marks can produce a regular variation between the two.

Then he began to create colour on the surface. This may look like paint or pastel but is a chemical process related to the patination of bronze. He has used two principal processes, the oxidisation of iron particles and a copper sulphate reaction: basically reddish and blue-green respectively, together with black (cement) and white (plaster). The red and blue are colours that appear only over a period and so are unlike applied paint; they vary according to the size of particles, the presence of water etc. For that reason the form of the carving on which they may lie can affect the colour: a hollow, for example, may gather and hold water and reagent and so deepen the tint. Cox's insistence on rebuilding the language of his art has led him to repudiate the current restrictive conditions of sculpture. But he may make use of any that are more distant and therefore less peremptory. This short account of his use of colour up to about 1983 shows him employing it in a way that may have owed something to the tradition of 'truth to materials', still very strong in modernism, but that tradition does not admit the painterly, decorative and even representational use of such colour in sculpture, however intrinsic to the support/medium. So Cox has used a process 'legitimate' to sculpture in a way considered 'illegitimate'.

Another limitation of modern sculpture which Cox was prepared to transgress was its repudiation of eroticism, at any rate of that which is not at once contradicted, confronted with irony, exacerbated by fetishism etc. Cox, beginning perhaps with the sensuality of rounded and polished stones, has followed the trail back to its analogies with rounded, coolly smooth skin. One work comprises three separate reliefs; in each, a part of the human body: shoulders, breasts, buttocks, all in a schematic form, is framed in undulating drapery, distinguished from the polished flesh by its whitish, scoured surface. Each panel is represented as if 'broken-off', by a region pitted with a pointed tool. The title 'Ecstasy: St. Agatha' refers to the martyred Christian saint whose breasts were cut off; the work itself reflects the ecstatic eroticism of certain Italian, especially Neapolitan, art. Such references are dangerous in their acceptance of a sensuality a little beyond what is acceptable in fine art.

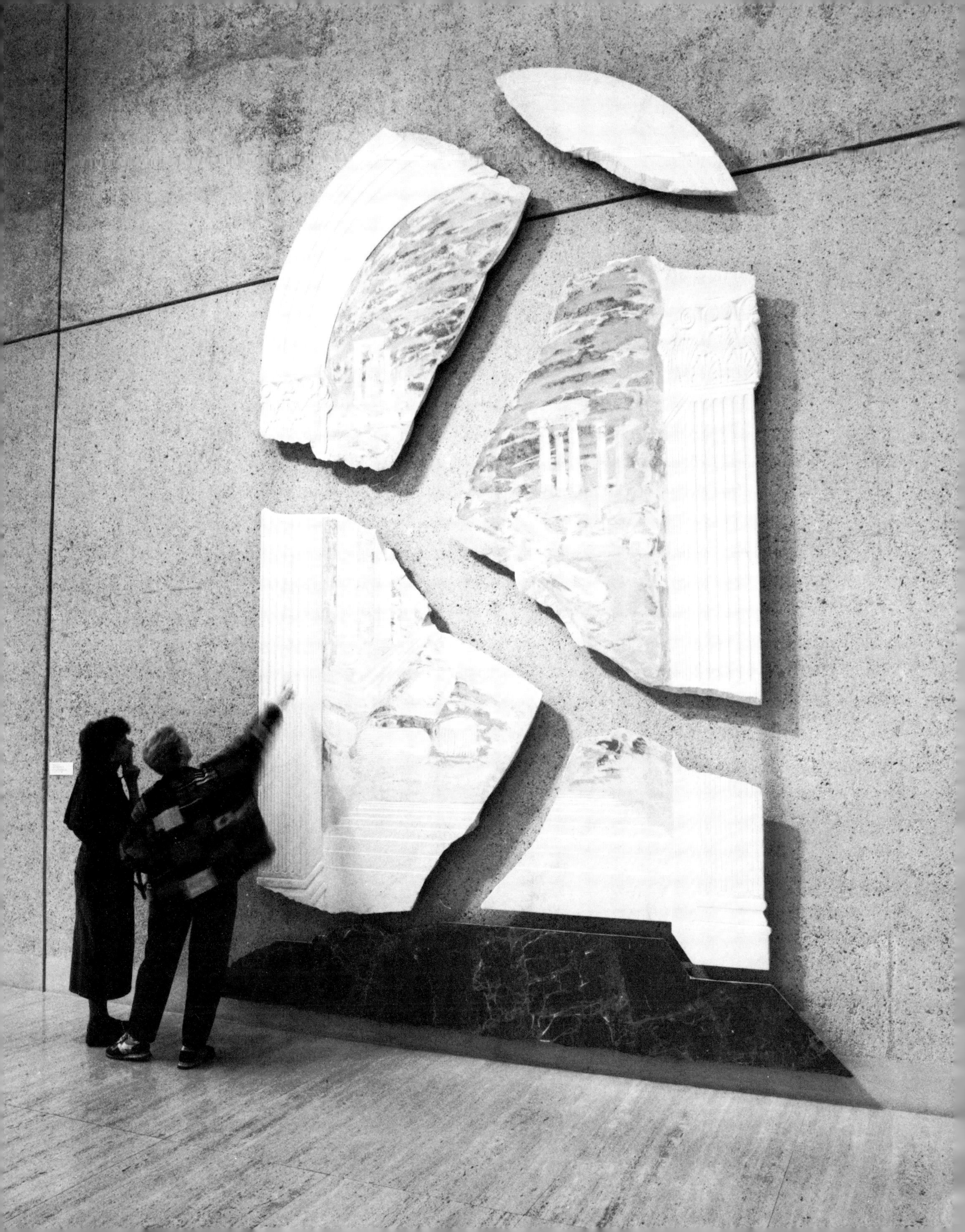

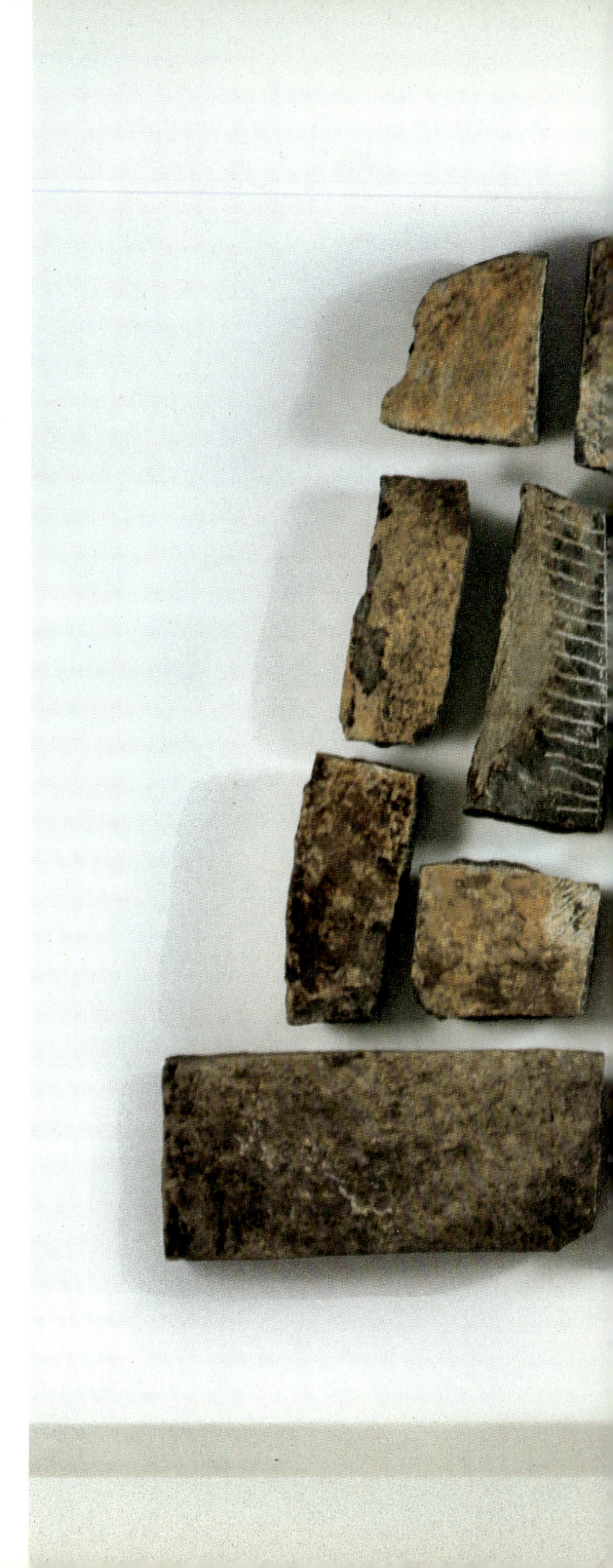

Rock Cut: Holy Family 1986
274 × 426 × 15 cm
Granite

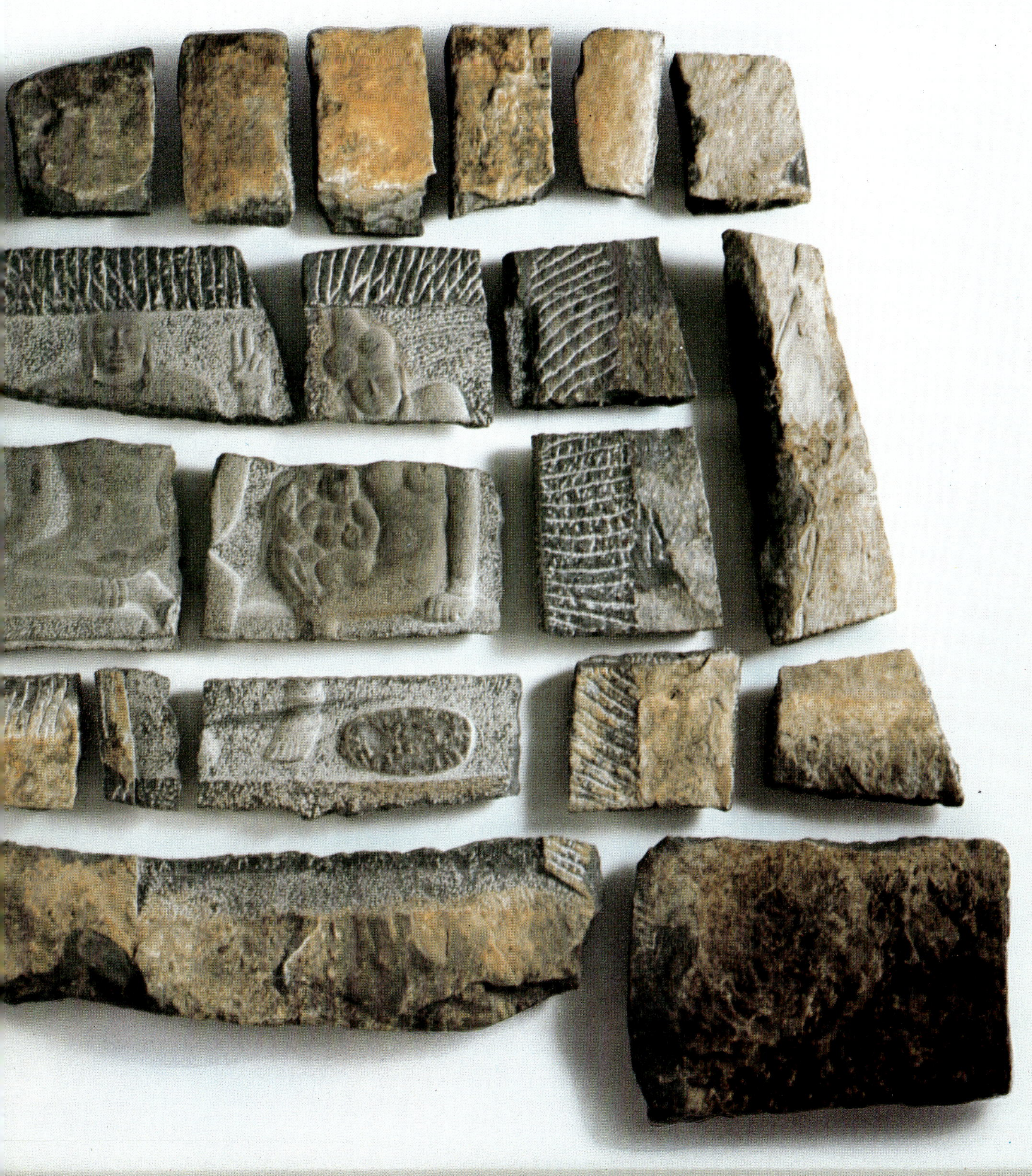

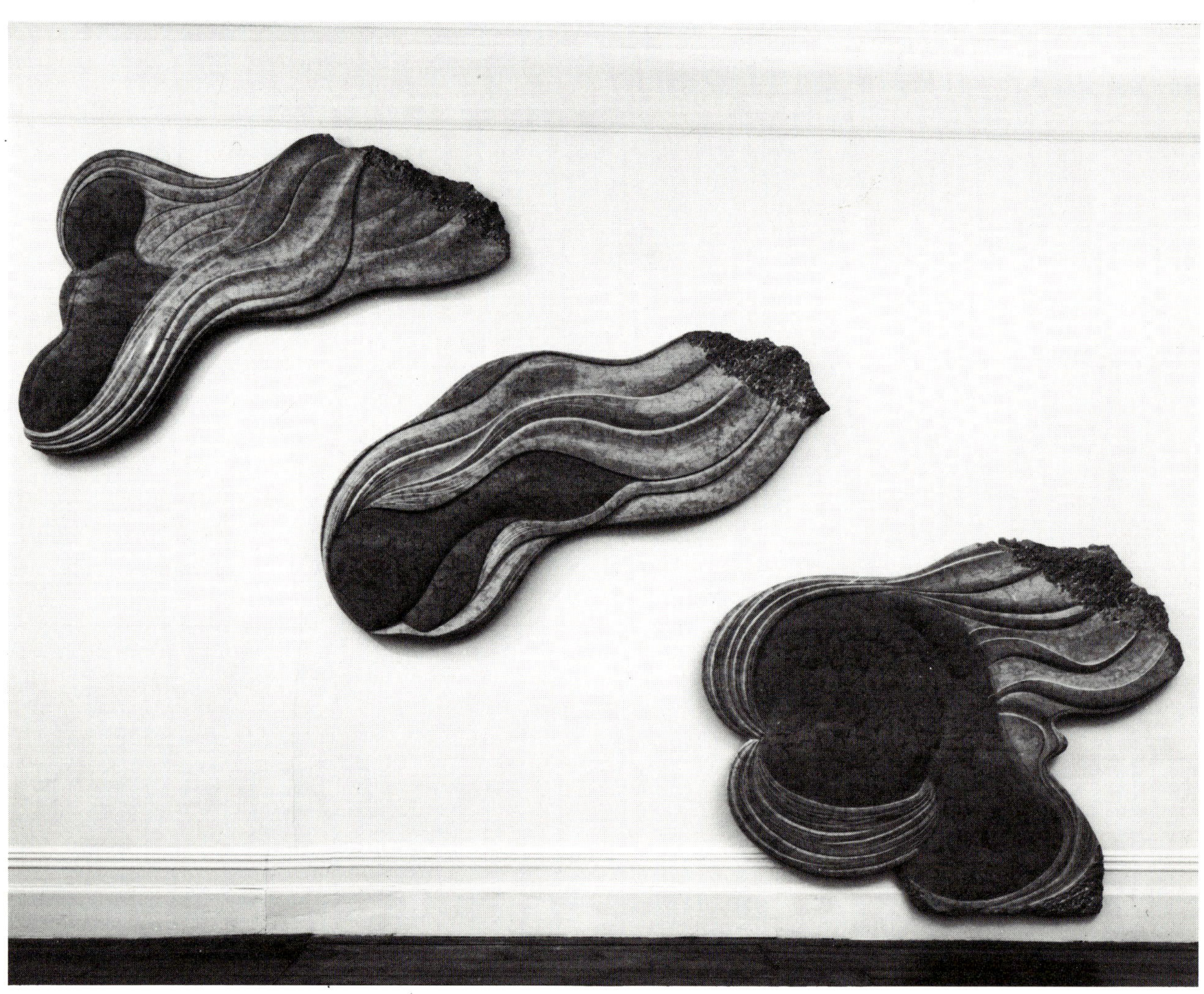

The reliefs achieve a decorative sensuousness that seems at first to reflect the excesses of Art-Nouveau decoration or of the extravagance of Baroque drapery, but finally declares its debt to the linear exuberance of a hero of his, Agostino di Duccio. This sculptor, who worked in Italy during the fifteenth century, especially in relief, was celebrated by Adrian Stokes and has been a fruitful influence on Cox.

A further reference is internal to Cox's sculptures – the analogy between the broken body and the 'broken' work of art. It is possible to account for the division of the body in this sculpture, however, in another way than by literal dismemberment. The three parts may be considered as three erogenous zones. Their separation, framing and anonymity (or depersonalisation) seems to correspond, with a hint of irony, to the overtones of the word 'zones'

The Fiery Kind 1983
110 × 130 cm
Rosso di Verona marble
The British Council

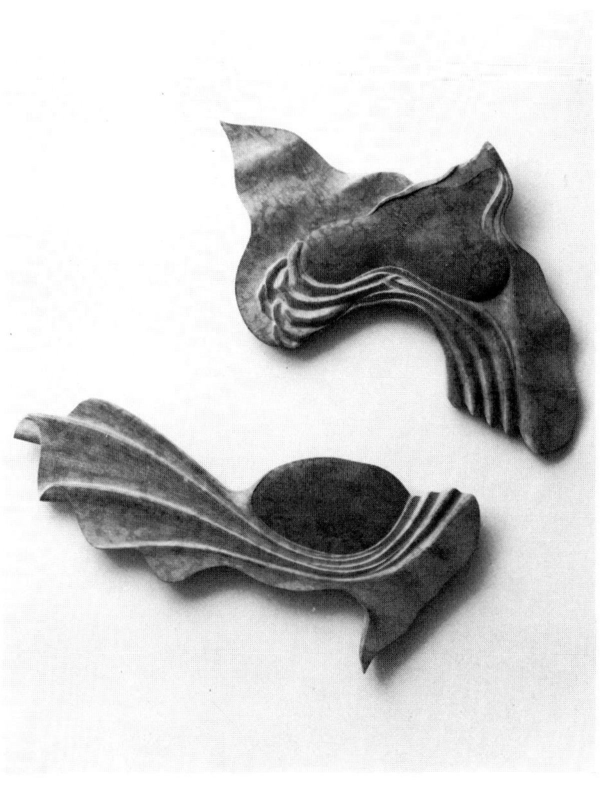

and also to the ambiguity of the word 'erogenous'. These are not the zones which are sensitive in the woman but rather those which excite the man who would possess the woman – by extension, the viewer of the work. The ambiguity is reinforced by comparison with the earlier four part work 'Figura Feminile Impudica' 1982 (a title borrowed from a Renaissance title meaning 'Immodest Female Figure'). Two of these, first and third, represent head and belly as smooth, featureless ovals; the second the breasts without nipples. In these the sensuality is essentially tactile and the absence of detail an inheritance of the reductive tradition of modern art. However, the fourth shows the thighs and the pubic region in profile, guarded by a small, sharp knife – an image remembered from a carving now in the Castello Sforzesca, Milan.

In the same year, Cox had begun to produce other works in which an apparently whole relief – marked as such by a geometric outline – is presented as having been broken and reassembled. No one meaning can be given to this feature which has been developed over several years. Formally it asserts that the wall is not only the physical support of the work but its field. The gaps are a means of fusing the architectural space with the created space within the work. The artist gives point to this, just as he

had in the reliefs of *c.* 1978, by constructing in terms of perspective, overlapping texture etc., a variety of spaces that make play with, extend or invade, the architectural ambience. Moreover the voids between the spaced-out fragments are used as elements in the composition, sometimes counterpointing or corresponding to drawn or carved elements.

I am tempted to see in the fragmentation and reconstruction an allegory of the fragmentation of modern art and of Cox's own personal reconstruction of it or even of his strategy of constructing an art out of the fragments of the art of the past. But more certainly, these works carry all the overtones of the basic meanings of construction and reconstruction, so fundamental to nature (for example, metamorphic rocks), to humanity and to art. As fragments, they represent Orwell's 'little chunk(s) of history that they have forgotten to alter', messages from the past (Orwell: *1984*). The exposed lines of breakage are also among the means by which Cox asserts the identity of his material and pays respect to the tradition in modern sculpture which values this assertion. They carry, moreover, secondary meanings; for example, reference to archaeological or geological reconstruction and exhibition. I believe that Cox is content to permit almost any structure of reference or reminiscence to be built upon his work. For example, you may consider looking at such a piece rather in the manner of a restorer or archaeologist wondering whether the artist has made a complete relief and broken it and then reconstructed or rearranged it again; whether he has broken and rearranged an unworked slab and then spread an image over it; or whether he has simply grouped together unrelated fragments of stone to use as the material of his art. The way in which you perceive these cases will affect your sense of the inflection of the whole metaphor. The clues, 'true' or 'false', that Cox provides are in terms of geometric versus irregular outline; continuity of pattern and repetition; matching or reversed correspondence of lines of cleavage (for a slab can be turned over after splitting); natural or artificial continuity or discontinuity of compositional lines and of represented objects, etc., etc. Plainly, as one becomes

Origin 1986
200 × 150 × 150 cm
Granite

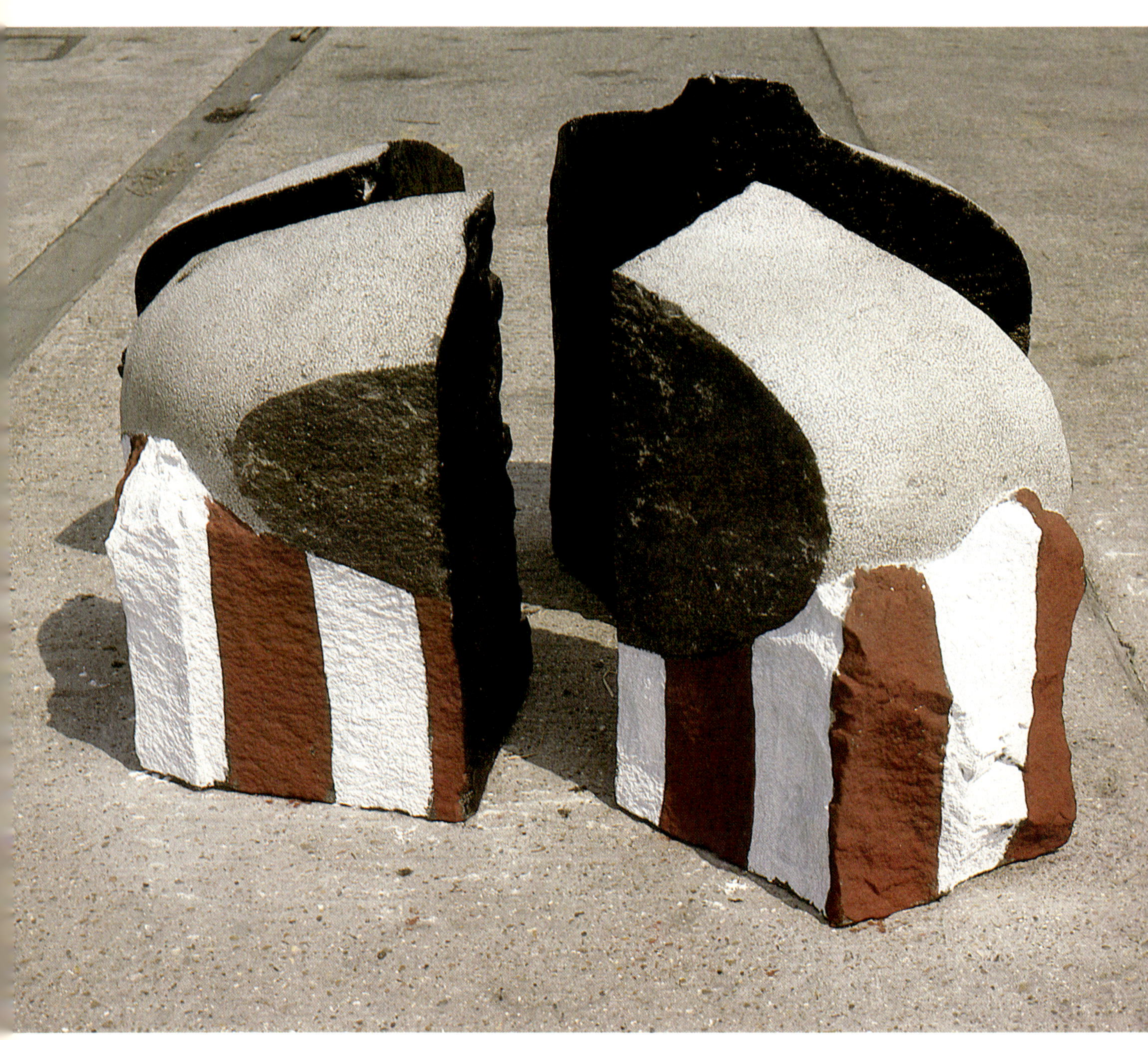

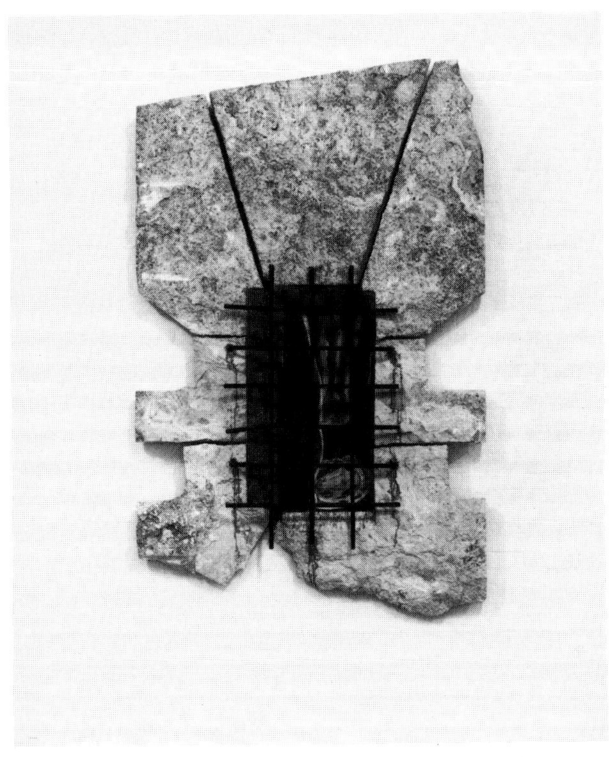

aware of all this, one becomes aware that such a device is not simply the expression of a nostalgia for the museum, a nostalgia for the art of the past or for irregularity itself, still less the manifestation of a psychic urge to destroy or dismember. Such associations may be almost unavoidable but I think they are more a part of his subject-matter than of the motivation of the artist himself; they are, in effect, acted as much as felt. Cox's view of creativity is not that it should be merely instinctive, emotional or, still less, incompatible with thought, but, rather, that it is strong enough to be able to live with, and flourish upon, contrivance and simulation. Only such a view is, perhaps, compatible with his ambition to comprehend the whole range of visual arts and this is even more clearly demonstrated by the range of his work in the last four years.

In the earliest of the broken and coloured pieces, 'Landscape with Ruins' 1982, architectural elements play three visible roles: first as support and field, then as a carved integral frame (the piece is represented as seen through an archway) and finally as the depicted element: a scattering of classical ruins on a hill-side. The implied subject is the range of Renaissance artists who practised painting, sculpture and architecture.

Perhaps as a means of controlling the power of the representation – especially of people – to disrupt archi-

tecture, he not only breaks the image into stony fragments and uses framing devices, but he softens, loosens and generalises the image itself. His reactive colour is, of course, not predictable enough to use in detail; the result is often like the airy style of some ancient Roman decoration. In addition, heads are generally featureless and bodies represented by a few loose-knit curves. Subject and material may also be cross-referenced. For example he may use the Travertine marble so typical of Roman architecture of all periods and represent on it a theme of the Church of Rome or he may quote from a familiar painting of the city of Rome by Turner.

Generally, in these works, the framing and distancing architecture will be classical and geometric. A recent series has engaged yet more closely with architecture; it is as if an architectural detail – a window – has been lifted from a sixteenth-century palace and transferred to the gallery. The type of window recreated is what is called rusticated – that is very rough-hewn so that it simulates the natural, uncut surfaces of un-dressed stone. One of these has an iron grille like those of a fortified palace, and through it you see, painted now in oil, a glimpse of a scene ambiguously of the present and past.

So Cox's art of sculpture is continually developing. He did not bring with him to India an inflexibly alien instrument, but one capable of growing by response to the rocks and to the human achievement that he finds. Above all, he shared with the Indian tradition, as well as with other old and rich traditions, a notion of a complex art: Architecture–Sculpture–Painting, with sculpture a degree dominant. The first results showed a return to a directly human theme: four heads emerging from granite slabs, as the crystals of the rock are burst, one at a time by the impact of a pointed tool. They represent the Four Senses: Taste, Sight, Hearing, Scent.

This group manifests in part a new interest in the cosmic formulations of alchemy, themselves a bridge between eastern and western thought, and between ancient and modern science. The title also implies an ecumenism. Cox imagined an ethnic link between India and the Mediterranean and associated it with the Etruscans

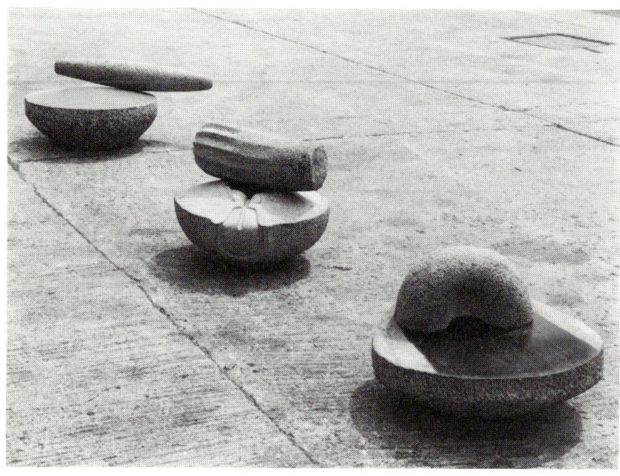

and their descendants in the isolated community of Viterbo, source of one of his most sensuous stones, Peperino.

A second set, larger in scale, comprises the five organs of understanding in the Samkhya philosophy. This doctrine, as summarised in a note on the Bhagavad-Gita, appeals to Cox as a theme, perhaps because, like early Renaissance perspective, but more generally, it offers a means of both realising and symbolising the cognitive basis of art and of human existence. The physical organs mediate the world to the perception of the mind (if I follow the doctrine) by corresponding to the gross elements: Earth (Smell – the nose), Water (Taste – the tongue), Fire (Sight – the eye), Air (Touch – the skin), Ether (Hearing – the ear) and, through them, the subtle elements, the 'Tanmatras' that underly them and which are themselves an emanation of mind. At the same time the work seems to synthesise signs of the three 'Gunas': 'Tamas' in the obduracy of the granite, 'Ragas' in the power and passion of the artist and 'Sattva' in the clarity of the form realised. The five senses are named according to the gross elements to which they correspond. They appear located on the ovals that (like others in his work) represent schematic heads but, at the same time, the egg of creation. The stone is polished and oiled so that the signs of its geological formation are revealed by an act of libation (puja).

It seems appropriate that Cox has gone back to a representation of creation and the physical origins of perception, by means of working in an ancient stone which has never been overlaid by sedimentation and which still dominates the structure of an ancient land.

The most significant part of that situation in which Cox created these works is the place itself, Mahabalipuram, a small town fifty kilometres from Madras that lies low on the coastal plain. The ground is sandy and from it rise several granite outcrops: a hill and huge rocks. Some of these have been carved into four small temples, the Rathas, archetypes of sacred design twelve hundred years ago, an elephant and a cow. The flank of the hill, a vast rounded boulder some fifty metres long is encrusted with figures in relief; gods, spirits, people, animals. Several portico temples are cut into the granite face of the hill, their back walls carved in over-life size relief. Another temple, built on rocks jutting out into the sea, is defended by a wall of caves. The style of all this sculpture of the seventh and eighth centuries is, compared with much other Indian art, informal, fresh, even a little ingenuous. The subjects, though theological, are realised rather as everyday life. A European is reminded of the vitality of the late middle ages and early Renaissance that were to come six hundred years later. But there is nothing in western sculpture that has this quality and yet is so grand, above all nothing that is integrated in the same way into the matrix of nature.

There is in western thought a pervasive dualism. Mind is set apart from nature. In Hinduism, since nature is a manifestation of spirit, it can be the direct expression of aspects of that spirit. There is no need of recourse to allegory. The western preoccupation with representation or illusion (in science as well as art) determines that drawing and painting have been our predominant visual arts. The Indian view (as I understand it) is that since nature itself is the illusion, the artist may create an equal reality by giving form, a form which corresponds to an immanent reality. The primary art is therefore sculpture. That sculpture is not set apart from nature but emerges from it as the surface is cut back. This is literally the case at Mahabalipuram but where, more often, the sculpture decorates a temple, it emerges from the structure of a building that has itself the character of a mountain or a cave.

Such an art fits perfectly the view that Cox had crystallised after reading Adrian Stokes, but it could be a formidable challenge for a visiting sculptor. He had the advantage of being able to work in the stoneyard of the

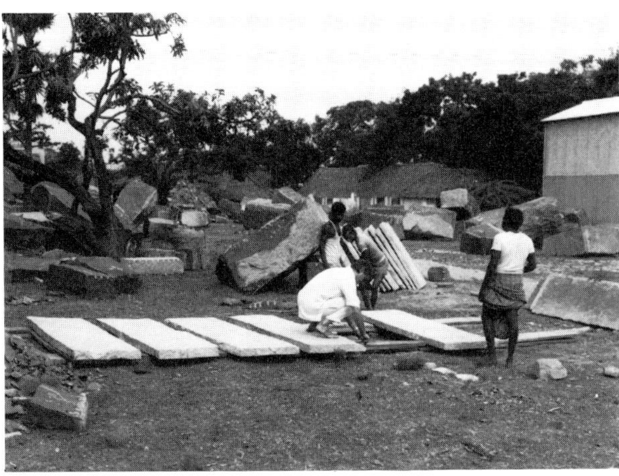

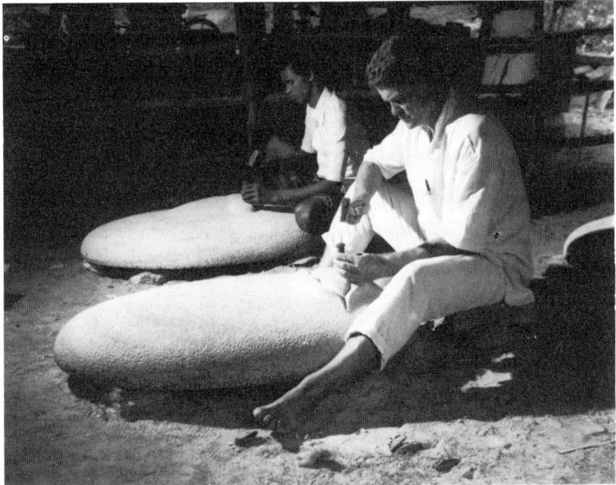

college which produces sculpture for Hindu temples that are erected all over the world.

The work is produced by the same techniques as that of the sculpture I have been describing but it has been formalised by long repetition. The college provides a powerful means of realising art, hands and eyes that inherit a rich tradition but no equally strong force of conceptual innovation that could deflect the intentions of a modern western sculptor, for that would be inappropriate to the tradition itself. The tradition is one of elaborating and adapting an existing repertory of forms. Cox found that his own work 'Etruscan' was quickly added to the repertory, being re-carved from a photograph in one of the stonecutters booths near the Rathas.

Stone is relatively cheap in Tamil Nadu, the carvers skilful and helpful. Cox could produce a great quantity of work in a short time. Such an opportunity is not often available for a carving sculptor. His exposure to Indian thought and culture filled his mind with ideas, at first,

naturally, evoked by the similarities and differences between the cultures, as he saw them. These led to some formal changes.

The 'Tanmatras' are arranged on the wall in a circle expressing the unity of the senses. Their oval form recalling that of the lingam, may imply that in Indian thought the senses are creative, not merely passive. This sets them apart from those works in which Cox had explored the possibilities of fragmentation. Two other great pieces, however, return to that theme. The figures of 'Rock Cut Holy Family' seem closer in type to the Hindu triad of Siva, Parvati and Skanda with their rather opulent physique. The raised fingers however suggest the heaven-pointing gesture of christian art. The substrate of granite fragments on which it is carved, though literally autochthonous, is disposed in a way that seems very western. It suggests the technique of building by setting one stone on another with its implied eventual ruination by dispersal rather than the Indian technique of carving out with its implied dissolution by erosion. Cox's own creative technique had involved fracture and dispersal. The Tamil process of powdering individual crystals that he was now using resembles erosion and part of the subject of the sculpture is that Indian technique. Represented on the separated stones is apparently the basic motif of a cell that is cut into the rock and the relief that is revealed on the back wall, a relief that could never be broken in the way that a relatively shallow applied relief could. The relief 'quoted' in this work is fuller than in other large scale works by Cox. In this rather subtle way the formal means as well as the nature of the representation express a fundamental difference between the traditions, even when they seem to be dealing with a closely related theme the sacred family as an expression of diversity in unity. At the same time they cross over and are themselves an expression of that same diversity in unity.

'Origin' seems to be the broken form of a stupa. In fact, partly assembled, partly riven, it is unified by the act of carving, by geometry of unity and by the associations of that geometry: the eclipse, the egg, the breast. The third large work: Domestic Rituals is in complete parts, each fully three dimensional, with no suggestion of fragmentation. Apparently quite different in mode to his predominant reliefs, this piece points up a long standing feature of Cox's work.

The granite from which the sculptured deities of Tamil Nadu are carved is also the material for countless grinding stones and querns. They can be seen stacked up for sale at the front of carving booths which take their place among the shops selling domestic wares in plastic and sheet metal. Cox has not so much represented but developed, heightened and recarved these forms. Such utensils are not common in the iconography of the western tradition, where, with exceptions, sculpture is distinguished from other types of artefact by the representation of the human form or animals. But of course the pestle and mortar, the grindstone and quern are themselves and have been for many hundreds of years a human representation. In Indian temples you may see rows of chapels each with its almost identical lingam and yoni in the form of pestle and mortar. It is the primary symbol of creativity. That is the subject of Cox's work and the theme of his development.

Milan

She speaks:

Let the earth of my body be mixed with the earth
my beloved walks on.
Let the fire of my body be the brightness
in the mirror that reflects his face.
Let the water of my body join the waters
of the lotus pool he bathes in.
Let the breath of my body be air
lapping his tired limbs.
Let me be sky, and moving through me
that cloud-dark Shyāma, my beloved.

From *In Praise of Krishna: Songs from the Bengali* trs. Edward C. Dimock Jnr. and Denise Levertov. Published by Jonathan Cape 1968.

Origin 1986
200 × 150 × 150 cm
Granite

Thousand Pillared Hall 1986
270 × 790 cm
Granite

Tanmatras 1985
304.8 × 304.8 × 22.9 cm
Granite

Rock Cut: Holy Family 1985
274.3 × 426.7 × 15.2 cm
Granite

Domestic Rituals 1985
a. 68.6 × 68.6 × 43.2 cm
b. 63.5 × 66 × 76.2 cm
c. 71.1 × 96.5 × 68.6 cm
Granite

Brides of Manamai 1986
435 × 240 × 4.35 cm
Granite, silk and mixed media

BIOGRAPHY

The Mediterranean is the womb of my civilisation, a limestone basin whose crustacea have accumulated and been thrust up to form mountains, vivacious, containing marble metamorphosed by compression: light, translucent, young enough to have memories to yield up.

The high places of Dravidia, says Forster, have faced the sun for longer than any other place on earth with 'forms that were his before our globe was torn from his bosom' (*A Passage to India*). Never submerged except as magma thrust up during the creation, its mountains atomised by millennia of baking wind, the source of India's ever swirling dust. Voluptuous, caressed, the shapes of landscape mirror its sculpture.

Man has defined his gods in this land where the closeness of the earth's crust lends little mystery to his origins, black hole or polished black granite. The navel of the cosmos realised in meditation. *Om* its first sound, light exposing form, the sculptor fashioning it. The gods live within the sculpture, within the stone where the answer has always lain regardless of its identity, Ganesh, Brahma, Siva, Vishnu, the hen that laid the 'Cosmic Egg' that floated in the Primal Waters.

Stephen Cox
Mahabalipuram 1985

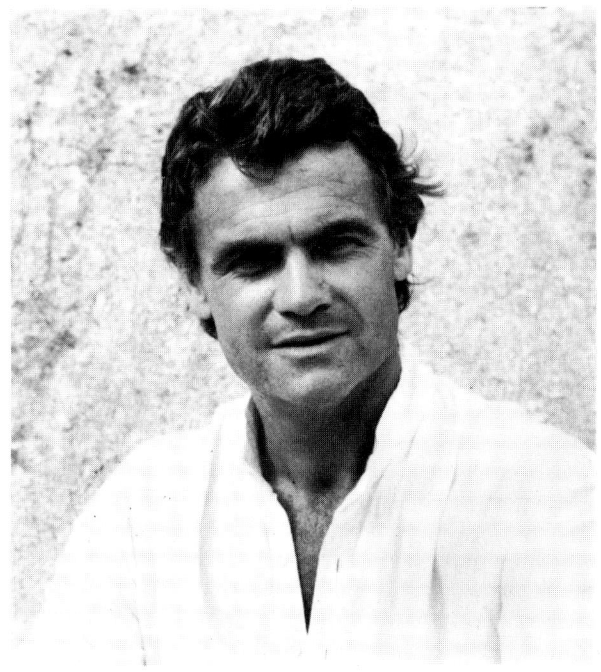

1946   Born in Bristol, England

SELECTED ONE-MAN EXHIBITIONS

1976 Lisson Gallery, London
1977 Lisson Gallery, London
1978 Galerie Swart, Amsterdam
1980 *Works 1970–80*, First Floor Lisson Gallery, London
1981 *Lunette*, Galleria Marilena Bonomo, Bari
Artra Studio, Milan
1982 Galleria La Salita, Rome
Spoleto Festival, Palazzo del Comune, Spoleto
1983 *Fragments from a Grand Tour: Italy 1981–83*, Nigel Greenwood Inc., London
Paesaggio: Rilievi 1982–83, Salone Villa Romana, Florence
1984 *Sketches and Modelli for 'Palanzana'*, Nigel Greenwood Inc., London
Casa di Masaccio, San Giovanni Valdarno
Galerie Eric Franck, Geneva
1985 *London International Contemporary Art Fair*, Tamarisk Gallery (Gibraltar)
We Must Always Turn South: Sculpture 1977–85, Arnolfini, Bristol

SELECTED GROUP EXHIBITIONS

1977 Fine Arts Building, New York
Julian Pretto Gallery, New York (installation)
Lisson Gallery, London
Whitechapel Art Gallery, London
Paris Biennale, Palais de Tokyo
1978 *Dessins en couleurs*, Gillespie De Laage, Paris
Lisson Gallery, London
Hayward Annual, Hayward Gallery, London
1979 Palais des Beaux Arts de Bruxelles (British/Belgian Art)
Pittura Ambiente, Palazzo Reale, Milan
Festival of Marble and Sound, Arandjelovac, Yugoslavia
1980 Lisson Gallery, London
Nuova Immagine, Milan Triennale, Palazzo del Arte
1981 *Enciclopedia*, Galleria Civica, Modena, Italy
Lisson Gallery, Summer Exhibition, London
British Sculpture in the 20th Century, Whitechapel Art Gallery, London
1982 *Generazioni a confronto*, University of Rome, Italy
Aperto '82, Venice Biennale, Italy
Englische Plastik Heute, Kunstmuseum Luzern, Switzerland
1983 *Codici e Marchingegni 1482–1983*, Castello dei Conti Guidi and Casa di Leonardo, Vinci, Italy
Tolly Cobbold Eastern Arts
The Sculpture Show, Hayward Gallery/Serpentine Gallery, London
New Art, Tate Gallery, London
'53–'83: Three Decades of Artists from Inner London Art Schools, Royal Academy of Arts, London

SELECTED BIBLIOGRAPHY

1984   *Sculpture New Directions*, Cleveland Gallery,
Middlesbrough
International Garden Festival, Liverpool
(sculpture commissioned by the Merseyside
Development Corporation and the Merseyside
County Council with the Arts Council of Great
Britain)
Twentieth Century Watercolours, Victoria &
Albert Museum, London
*An International Survey of Recent Painting and
Sculpture*, Museum of Modern Art, New York
*5 Scultori inglesi: Cox, Cragg, Houshiary, Kapoor,
Woodrow*, Artra Studio, Milan

1985   *The British Show*, British Council exhibition
touring Australia
Sculptors Drawings, Scottish Arts Council
Touring exhibition
Intorno Flauto Magico, Palazzo della
Permanente, Milan
The 4th Henry Moore Grand Prize Exhibition,
The Utsukushi-ga-hara Open-air Museum,
Japan
Anni Ottanta, Ravenna.

1986   *Forty Years of Modern Art 1945–85*,
Tate Gallery, London

1986   *Sixth Indian Triennale*, Delhi

1986   *Arte e Alchimia*, XLII Biennale D: Venezia

1986   *Origins, Originality and Beyond*, The Biennale of
Sydney

1986   *Prospekt 86*, Kunstverein, Frankfurt

John McEwen: 'Miscellany', *The Spectator*,
10 December 1977
Peter Smith: review in *Studio International*, no. 1,
London, 1977
Richard Cork: review in *The Guardian*, 24 August 1977
Michael Compton: in catalogue, 10th Paris Biennale,
1977
Simon Vaughan-Winter: review in *Artscribe*, no. 10,
1978
Art Actuel, Skira Annuel 78, Geneva, 1978
Sarah Kent: 'Stephen Cox' in catalogue, *Hayward
Annual*, 1978
William Packer: review in *Financial Times*,
5 September, 1978
Juliet Steyn: review in *Art Monthly*, no. 19, 1978
Stephen Cox: (Statements) in catalogue, Galerie Swart,
Amsterdam, 1978
Sarah Kent: review in *Time Out*, September 1978
John McEwen: 'Beleaguered', *The Spectator*, September
1978
Sandy Nairne: 'Au sujet de l'oeuvre de S. Cox,
B. Flanagan, P. Joseph, B. Law, G. Onwin et
D. Tremlett' in catalogue, *JP2*, Palais des Beaux-Arts
de Bruxelles, 1979
Bernard Marcellis: 'Un Certain art anglais, Paris &
Bruxelles', *Domus*, Milan, June 1979
Suzi Gablik: 'The Uncoring of Abstract Art', *Harpers &
Queen*, October 1979
Flavio Caroli: *Enciclopedia*, Modena 1981
Santa Fizzarotti: 'Stephen Cox, Galleria Bonomo, Bari';
Segno 21, Pescara, June 1981
Loredana Parmesani: 'Stephen Cox, Artra Studio
Milano', *Flash Art*, Italian edition no. 106,
December/January 1982
Flavio Caroli: 'Il cemento diventa prezioso', *Corriere
della Sera*, Milan, 25 November 1981
Fabrizio d'Amico: 'La pietra ferita di Cox', *La
Repubblica*, Roma, 28 February 1982
Flavio Caroli: *Magico primario: l'Arte degli anni ottanta*,
Ed. Fabbri, Milan, 1982

Giovanni Carendente: *Stephen Cox*, catalogue, Festival de Due Mondi, Spoleto, 1982

Martin Kunz: 'Neue Skulptur am Beispiel englischer Künstler', *Kunst Bulletin*, no. 6, Berne, June 1982

Fabrizio d'Amico: *'Cox und der verwundete Stein*/Cox and the Wounded Stone', in catalogue, Kunstmuseum Luzern, 1982

Martin Kunz: 'Englische Kunst heute' in catalogue, *British Sculpture Now*, Kunstmuseum Luzern, 1982

Simonetta Lux: 'Stephen Cox, Galleria la Salita', *Flash Art*, May 1982

Marina Vaizey: 'England Takes the Honours', *The Sunday Times*, 13 June 1982

Sarah Kent: review in *Time Out*, 22 April 1983

Marina Vaizey: 'Playing Serious Games', *The Sunday Times*, 24 April 1983

William Feaver: 'Salvage into Sculpture', *The Observer*, 24 April 1983

John Russell Taylor: 'Hidden Talent in the Second Division', *The Times*, 26 April 1983

John McEwen: 'Pathfinders', *The Spectator*, 30 April 1983

Juliet Steyn: 'Stephen Cox', *Art Monthly*, no. 66, May 1982

Sandro Vezzozi: foreword in catalogue, *Codici e Marchingegni*, Vinci, Italy

Simon Vaughan Winter: 'Stephen Cox', *Artscribe*, no. 41, June 1983

Helen Drysdale: 'The Sculpture Show', *Artscribe*, no. 42, July 1983

Catalogue, *The Sculpture Show*, Hayward and Serpentine Galleries, August–October 1983

Catalogue, *New Art*, Tate Gallery, September–October 1983

Catalogue, *'53–'83, Three Decades of Artists from Inner London Art Schools*, Royal Academy, ILEA publication, 1983

William Feaver: 'The New British Sculpture', *Art News*, vol. 83, no. 1, January 1984

Peter Davies: *Sculpture – New Directions*, catalogue, Cleveland Gallery, Middlesbrough, 1983

Caroline Collier: 'Stephen Cox', *Flash Art*, no. 118, Summer 1984

John Russell Taylor: 'Stephen Cox', *The Times*, 8 May 1984

Sarah Kent: 'Stephen Cox', *Time Out*, 17 May 1984

Front cover (Installation photograph, Nigel Greenwood Gallery): *Art Monthly*, no. 77, June 1984

Kynaston McShine: *An International Survey of Recent Painting and Sculpture*, catalogue, Museum of Modern Art, New York, 1984

Giovanni Carendente: *Stephen Cox*, catalogue, San Giovanni, Valdarno, Italy, published by Carini, November 1984

'Le Grand tour de Cox', *Tribune de Geneve*, 16 November 1984

Catalogue, group exhibition, Galleria Chisel, Genoa, November 1984

Catalogue, *The British Show*, touring exhibition, British Council, Australia 1985

Charlotte Haenlein: 'Stephen Cox: Eine neue Perspektive in der britischen Skulptur', *Du*, October 1985

Ronnie Rees, Sarah Kent, *We Must Always Turn South*, catalogue, Arnolfini Gallery, 1985

Michael Compton, *Stephen Cox*, catalogue, Triennale of India, The British Council, 1986

Flavio Caroli, *Origins, Originality and Beyond*, catalogue, Biennale of Sydney, 1986

Sarah Kent, *Something to Say*

Arturo Schwarz, *Arte e Alchimia*, catalogue, Biennale di Venezia, 1986